7 Absolutes To Pray Over Your Kids

by Blaine Bartel

Harrison House
Tulsa, Oklahoma

09 08 07 06 05   10 9 8 7 6 5 4 3 2 1

7 Absolutes To Pray Over Your Kids
ISBN 1-57794-734-7
Copyright © 2005 by Blaine Bartel
P.O. Box 691923
Tulsa, Oklahoma 74179

Published by Harrison House, Inc.
P.O. Box 35035
Tulsa, Oklahoma 74153

Contents

Introduction

After ministering to children and teenagers for over twenty years and raising three of our own, my wife, Cathy, and I can tell you that there is nothing too hard for God—but you have to pray! We pray for our kids on a regular basis, but we don't have a set ritual or meeting time. Prayer is part of our family life. We pray as a couple, we pray as a family, and we pray for each other as the Holy Spirit leads us during the day. But one day I sat down and asked the Lord to show me the principles that He had us praying for kids all these years. That is when He revealed seven powerful absolutes to pray over kids.

If you are a parent, you have a love and a concern for your kids. You want to help them to excel, to pursue greatness, and to enjoy life as they do exploits for God. While you are helping them along the way, I encourage you to take this book and pray these seven principles over them. The Word of God tells us that prayer is what moves mountains and calms storms, so praying for your kids is one of the most important things you can do to assist them in life.

You might be saying, "This is totally irrelevant to my life. I don't have kids and never plan to have them." So I challenge you: has there never been a kid in your life? Every human being deals with kids, whether you actually parent them or not. If you are young, you may change your mind later and have kids. But even if you don't, as you grow older your brothers and sisters will have kids. Your friends will have kids. When you go to church, you are around kids. The people in your neighborhood or apartment building have kids. And no matter what your relationship is with those kids in your life, you can have a tremendous impact on their lives by simply praying for them.

Maybe your kids are grown and are rebellious toward you and toward God. As far as you can see, nothing you say or do affects their thinking or behavior. If that is the case, then this book is also for you. *They* may not listen to you, but *God* does! Start praying these prayers and principles over their lives, and believe God to move your kids into right relationship with God and with you.

And don't leave yourself out! The principles I share and the prayers I teach in this book are just as effective for *you* as they are for the kids you pray for. You can practice these principles and pray these prayers for yourself, then see tremendous benefits in your own life—but there's much more.

The greatest joy in the Christian life is praying for someone and seeing their life transformed by the love and power of God. That is the adventure you enter into when you begin to pray for your own children, for the teenagers down the street who drive you crazy, for that nephew or niece that needs a miracle, or that grandchild who is in rebellion. Personally, I have seen many miracles because a parent or grandparent—or a neighbor or teacher—prayed for a young person.

One of the greatest impacts you can make on the next generation will happen because you prayed for them. If you are dissatisfied with the world in which you live; if you have problems with your own kids or the kids "coming up" in your church or on your block; then it's time for you to learn and pray the *7 Absolutes To Pray Over Your Kids.*

1

Wisdom

Wisdom is the principal thing; Therefore get wisdom.

Proverbs 4:7

The Bible tells us that wisdom is the most important thing a believer can have. Therefore, we should pray first that our kids have wisdom. If they are wise, everything else falls into place. So we are going to take a good, long look at wisdom because we want our kids to be successful in every area of their lives.

I don't know about you, but I'm results oriented. I'm competitive. I want to win. When I do something, I like to see the fruit of it. And I'm the same way about prayer. When I pray for my own kids and other kids, I do my best to see that I am praying according to God's Word and His will because I want to see my prayers answered. I want to see their lives touched and changed by God, to see them walk in His ways and power. Bottom line is: I want my prayers to work.

As parents and mentors of kids, we know that one of the best ways to discover prayers that work is to read the Bible and find out whose prayers were answered and what they prayed. What wisdom did they walk in? An example of someone who prayed and got results was Hannah in the Old Testament. In 1 Samuel, chapter 1, she prayed because she had a problem with her kids: she didn't have any!

Hannah's Prayer

Then Elkanah her husband said to her, "Hannah, why do you weep? Why do you not eat? And why is your heart grieved? Am I not better to you than ten sons?"

So Hannah arose after they had finished eating and drinking in Shiloh. Now Eli the priest was sitting on the seat by the doorpost of the tabernacle of the Lord.

And she was in bitterness of soul, and prayed to the LORD and wept in anguish.

Then she made a vow and said, "O Lord of hosts, if You will indeed look on the affliction of Your

maidservant and remember me, and not forget Your
maidservant, but will give Your maidservant a male
child, then I will give him to the Lord all the days
of his life, and no razor shall come upon his head."

1 Samuel 1:8-11

Every year Elkanah and his family journeyed to
Shiloh, where the tabernacle or tent of worship stood.
Like the rest of Israel, they came to pray, offer sacrifices, and worship God. Hannah was "in bitterness of
soul" because she had no children. She and Elkanah
had tried and tried, but she remained barren, so she
poured out her heart to God. She promised Him that
if He gave her a son, she would dedicate him to His
service and see that he lived a holy life.

And it happened, as she continued praying before
the Lord, that Eli watched her mouth.
Now Hannah spoke in her heart; only her lips
moved, but her voice was not heard. Therefore Eli
thought she was drunk.
So Eli said to her, "How long will you be drunk?
Put your wine away from you!"

1 Samuel 1:12-14

Eli was the High Priest who officiated over the
affairs of the tabernacle, helping the people of God

with their sacrifices and hearing their prayers. As Hannah prayed, he watched her. He saw her mouth move, but no words were spoken, so Eli thought that she had been drinking. He accused her of being drunk in the Lord's tabernacle and told her to clean up her act!

Hannah immediately denied that she was drunk and explained her situation to Eli.

> But Hannah answered and said, "No, my lord, I am a woman of sorrowful spirit. I have drunk neither wine nor intoxicating drink, but have poured out my soul before the Lord.
>
> Do not consider your maidservant a wicked woman, for out of the abundance of my complaint and grief I have spoken until now."
>
> Then Eli answered and said, "Go in peace, and the God of Israel grant your petition which you have asked of Him."
>
> And she said, "Let your maidservant find favor in your sight." So the woman went her way and ate, and her face was no longer sad.
>
> 1 Samuel 1:15-18

Eli told her that she could be at peace because God had heard her prayers, and He was going to grant her petition.

It didn't matter how Hannah prayed, that she didn't yell in a booming voice or even say anything out loud. God heard her heart, and He hears yours too. Also, it is interesting that one of the first things the devil tried to do as Hannah was praying for a child was to demean and devalue her. Through Eli's accusation that she was drunk, the enemy attempted to bring condemnation on her. He also tried to cause a serious misunderstanding between her and the man of God.

Satan hates it when you pray for kids. He will do everything he can to convince you that you are a "nobody" to God and that God doesn't care about you or your kids. He will get other people to criticize you and make you feel unworthy of God's attention. He'll try to talk you out of praying; and if he can't talk you out of it, he'll introduce every lie he can think of to get you to believe that your prayers are completely ineffective. Basically, he wants you to fall into doubt and discouragement and then quit praying altogether.

Hannah never stopped praying, and she had the wisdom to tell Eli exactly what she was praying for and what her situation was when he accused her of being drunk. Then Eli heard from God and put her heart at ease that her prayers had been heard and answered. By the time she left the tabernacle, she was a changed woman. Hannah had come to Shiloh broken, but her faith in God caused her to pour out her heart in prayer. After talking with the priest, she returned home full of hope and expectancy.

Doing Your Part

> Then they rose early in the morning and worshiped before the Lord, and returned and came to their house at Ramah. And Elkanah knew Hannah his wife, and the Lord remembered her.
>
> So it came to pass in the process of time that Hannah conceived and bore a son, and called his name Samuel, saying, "Because I have asked for him from the Lord."
>
> 1 Samuel 1:19,20

The Bible says that God granted Hannah's petition, but she and Elkanah still had to do their part! In most cases, when you petition the Lord, He will give you steps to take or further prayers to pray regarding the situation. In other words, when you're praying for your kids, that's not where it stops. You don't just pray, "God, I need my kids to stop fighting and bickering," and then never discipline them, instruct them, and teach them what the Word of God has to say about anger and strife. God can only do so much if you are not training your children according to His Word and being led by His Spirit.

You're probably thinking, *Well, what's the point of praying for that kid next door if his parents just let him run wild?* Pray for his parents too! Pray for opportunities to speak into their lives. And remember, nothing is too hard for God. Doing your part means praying first, then looking for that open door to influence them toward looking to Jesus and living godly lives.

Hannah prayed, and then she did her part. Elkanah "knew" Hannah and she conceived and gave birth to a son. That was such a great day! She and Elkanah named their son Samuel, which means "heard of God."[1] This name indicated that he was God's answer to prayer. Therefore, every time they called his name, they reminded him and themselves that God answered their prayers. Whenever they said, "Samuel, come over here," they were really saying, "Answer To Prayer, come over here! Heard Of God, take out the garbage!"

God Turns a Nation

Hannah kept her word to God and raised Samuel to love and serve Him. As soon as he was weaned, she brought him to Eli for the Lord's service, but every year she would visit him and remind him of his consecration to God. That was a good thing because Samuel lived with Eli, and it wasn't the godliest environment.

> Then Elkanah went to his house at Ramah. But the child ministered to the Lord before Eli the priest.
>
> Now the sons of Eli were corrupt; they did not know the Lord.
>
> 1 Samuel 2:11,12

Eli had assistants in the tabernacle, and two of those assistants were his own sons. The problem was that they did not know the Lord or have respect for His ways, and they were doing all kinds of abominable things in God's house. They were supposed to be assisting their father, helping people with their sacrifices and leading people in their worship of God, but they were corrupt. They abused the meat sacrifices, forcing people to give them up for their personal consumption, and they had sex with prostitutes right in the tabernacle!

I'm sure Eli didn't set out to make his sons wicked, ungodly men. We never see in the Bible where Eli said, "Hey, come on over here, guys. I want to show you this nasty stuff on the Internet. Here's a *Playboy* magazine I want you to read. And I got you some pot to smoke because I want you to try to have sex with all the prostitutes and hurt as many people of God as you can."

Eli never encouraged his sons to sin or turn away from God. Do you know what he did? He ignored them. You don't have to introduce your children to sin to get them into sin. All you have to do is stand back and not deal with them. Ignore the issues in their lives, the problem areas. Then they will practice sin on their own.

> Foolishness is bound up in the heart of a child; The rod of correction will drive it far from him.
>
> Proverbs 22:15

Eli may have prayed for his sons to grow up and serve God, but unlike Hannah and Elkanah, he did not discipline and teach them. If we let our kids grow up without correction, discipline, instruction, help, and guidance; they will find foolish things to do. And it doesn't matter if we are in full-time ministry. It doesn't matter if we are a priest, a prophet, a king, a wealthy businessman, or a president. Our position doesn't matter when it comes to raising and influencing kids. If we don't take time with them and pray for them, they will turn out just like Eli's sons: corrupt, wicked, and not knowing or serving the Lord.

> Therefore the sin of the young men [Eli's sons] was very great before the Lord, for men abhorred the offering of the Lord.
>
> But Samuel ministered before the Lord, even as a child, wearing a linen ephod.
>
> Moreover his mother used to make him a little robe, and bring it to him year by year when she came up with her husband to offer the yearly sacrifice.
>
> 1 Samuel 2:17,18 [insert mine]

Hannah kept her promise to the Lord, even though it must have been hard to give Samuel up at such a young age. She saw him once a year when she and Elkanah came to worship at the tabernacle, and she would always bring him a new robe that she had made for him. The robe was a priestly garment, indicating that she was involved in his spiritual preparation and training. It also reminded Samuel and everyone else that Samuel's life was dedicated to the Lord's service.

Samuel grew up learning the customs of the tabernacle and what it meant to be part of the priesthood. Eli and the other priests mentored and discipled him. And every year, his parents would come to reinforce his dedication to the Lord. Although Samuel was surrounded by the corruption of Eli's sons and saw how they continuously defiled the tabernacle of God, he turned out right. Although he was raised mostly by Eli, the prayers and influence of his parents overcame the evil around him.

What a miracle this was! In the midst of tremendous wickedness, God raised up a priest who would be one of the most powerful and respected in Israel's history—all because of a mother's prayers.

> Now this shall be a sign to you that will come upon your two sons, on Hophni and Phinehas: in one day they shall die, both of them.
>
> Then I will raise up for Myself a faithful priest who shall do according to what is in My heart and in My mind. I will build him a sure house, and he shall walk before My anointed forever.
>
> 1 Samuel 2:34,35

For years Israel had gone downhill under Eli's spiritual leadership. His sons had desecrated the tabernacle and maligned the priesthood, but then a little woman named Hannah prayed for a son. Her prayers and the influence of Hannah and Elkanah brought forth a godly leader to turn Israel around. God used Samuel in a mighty way as a godly priest, a godly judge, and a godly prophet.

The hinges of history hang on the prayers of mothers and fathers over kids!

Walk in Wisdom

It is God's absolute will for our kids to walk in wisdom just as Samuel walked in wisdom. He wants them to be "bright and brighter" not "dumb and dumber"! He wants them to know what to do and how to do it. And there is a good reason for that. The most important decisions people make in life are made when they are just kids.

Your kids are going to decide who their friends are, what career they will pursue, where they will go to school, whom they will marry, where they will live, and what church they will attend. These are major decisions that will affect the rest of their lives, and they need God's wisdom.

The important decisions kids make can get parents completely freaked out if they don't turn to God's Word and begin to pray! In the book of Ephesians, Paul prayed a prayer that we can pray for our children and for every kid in our life who needs wisdom.

> Therefore I also, after I heard of your faith in the Lord Jesus and your love for all the saints, do not cease to give thanks for you, making mention of you in my prayers: that the God of our Lord Jesus Christ, the Father of glory, may give to you the spirit of wisdom and revelation in the knowledge of Him.
>
> Ephesians 1:15-17

Paul said, "Listen, I'm praying for you, Ephesians. I'm praying that God will give you a spirit of wisdom and revelation in the knowledge of Jesus Christ." He didn't pray for them to be smart or for their IQ to go up thirty points. He prayed that they would have God's wisdom and revelation, supernatural discernment and insight, regarding the affairs of life.

Paul knew and we must realize that it is not enough for our kids to have great book knowledge.

That is important, but without wisdom they will not know how to rightly apply the information and knowledge that they have gained.

Knowledge is the accumulation of facts and truths, but wisdom is the correct and proper application of those facts and truths. You can have all the facts and information, but if you don't apply them in your everyday experience, you can make a mess of your life. You will make bad decisions and get into trouble.

It is interesting that Samuel anointed David and greatly influenced him when he was a kid. Then David had a son, Solomon, who was known for his wisdom. In fact, when David died and Solomon became king, God told young Solomon that He would grant him whatever he asked for. What was Solomon's deepest desire?

> Now give me wisdom and knowledge, that I may go out and come in before this people; for who can judge this great people of Yours?"
>
> 2 Chronicles 1:10

Solomon asked for wisdom and knowledge! And from this passage of Scripture we see how much God valued Solomon's choice.

Then God said to Solomon: "Because this was in your heart, and you have not asked riches or wealth or honor or the life of your enemies, nor have you asked long life—but have asked wisdom and knowledge for yourself, that you may judge My people over whom I have made you king—

wisdom and knowledge are granted to you; and I will give you riches and wealth and honor, such as none of the kings have had who were before you, nor shall any after you have the like."

2 Chronicles 1:11,12

God was extremely impressed that Solomon asked for wisdom and not riches, power, fame, or even a long life. He was so impressed that He gave Solomon all that too! Obviously, King David and Bathsheba had prayed for their son and had taught him well to value wisdom.

We need to pray for our kids to have the wisdom to apply what they know. Then, like Solomon, God can bless them with success in every area of their lives.

Following is a prayer that you can pray, asking God for your kids to have wisdom. Again, if you don't have kids of your own, I am sure there are some kids in your life who could use wisdom, and your prayers can have a profound effect on their lives.

Prayer for Wisdom

Father, in the name of Jesus, we thank You for giving our children a spirit of wisdom and revelation in the knowledge of You. We believe that their heads are covered with the helmet of salvation, and that they have the mind of our Lord, Jesus Christ. We pray that our children will make intelligent, informed, and Spirit-inspired decisions today and every day. Father, please give them supernatural discernment and a godly evaluation of every situation they encounter. And surround them with counselors who abide in Your Word and walk according to Your Spirit. In Jesus' name we pray, amen.

2

Protection

But know this, that in the last days perilous times will come:

For men will be lovers of themselves, lovers of money, boasters, proud, blasphemers, disobedient to parents, unthankful, unholy,

unloving, unforgiving, slanderers, without self-control, brutal, despisers of good,

traitors, headstrong, haughty, lovers of pleasure rather than lovers of God,

having a form of godliness but denying its power.

2 Timothy 3:1-5

We live in a pretty dangerous world today, but this time of terror did not take God by surprise. He knew we would live in a crazy world of weirdos, perverts, terrorists, bad drivers—even mad cows! He knew that you would be hesitant to let your kids go out the door into such a world. Therefore, in this day and hour of history, it is especially important to pray for our kids' protection. As believers living in a very challenging time, we must know how to pray and what to pray to see the next generation grow up and stay strong in God.

God's Supernatural Safety

Jesus was a tremendous example of someone who prayed and then walked in His Father's protection. If there was ever one individual in the world that the devil wanted to take out early, it was Jesus. Satan did everything he could to try to kill Jesus from the time He was born, and he never stopped trying until after the crucifixion. At the very beginning of Jesus' ministry, as He began to preach and teach the gospel, Satan incited the crowd to try to kill Him.

> So all those in the synagogue, when they heard these things, were filled with wrath,
>
> and rose up and thrust Him out of the city; and they led Him to the brow of the hill on which their city was built, that they might throw Him down over the cliff.
>
> Then passing through the midst of them, He went His way.
>
> Luke 4:28-30

Jesus walked right through the crowd to safety! It was like all his enemies became suddenly blind or He disappeared from their sight. As we read through the gospels we see how He had God's supernatural protection again and again.

I believe God can and will protect our kids in the same way He protected Jesus, but we have a part to play. We must pray.

The Supernatural Influence of Prayer

> Therefore I exhort first of all that supplications, prayers, intercessions, and giving of thanks be made for all men,
>
> for kings and all who are in authority, that we may lead a quiet and peaceable life in all godliness and reverence.
>
> 1 Timothy 2:1,2

In these verses Paul gives us a big hint about how to have the protection of God in our lives and the lives of our kids. He tells us to pray and thank God for ALL men, meaning all human beings, as well as for kings and those in authority over our lives.

We should be praying for our spiritual leaders, our kids' teachers in school, our government officials and judges, and even the guys who pick up our garbage twice a week. When we do that, we lead a "quiet and peaceable life." This tells us that God is honoring our prayers and turning the hearts of not only those in authority over us, but also "all men" who touch our lives and our kids' lives. These are the people who determine whether we live in quiet and peace or conflict and distress.

You can create a spiritual environment around kids by praying that wherever they go, they will encounter the proper influences they need to discern God's will and make the right decisions. Right decisions keep them safe. You can pray for laborers to come across their path, who will share God's Word with them in a meaningful and relevant way. You can pray for them to hear the gospel and receive Jesus if they have not been saved yet. After all, real protection begins with their eternal security in Christ Jesus.

Safe in the Family of God

When Jesus came into the region of Caesarea Philippi, He asked His disciples, saying, "Who do men say that I, the Son of Man, am?"

So they said, "Some say John the Baptist, some Elijah, and others Jeremiah or one of the prophets."

He said to them, "But who do you say that I am?"

Simon Peter answered and said, "You are the Christ, the Son of the living God."

Jesus answered and said to him, "Blessed are you, Simon Bar-Jonah, for flesh and blood has not revealed this to you, but My Father who is in heaven.

And I also say to you that you are Peter, and on this rock I will build My church, and the gates of Hades shall not prevail against it.

And I will give you the keys of the kingdom of heaven, and whatever you bind on earth will be bound in heaven, and whatever you loose on earth will be loosed in heaven."

Matthew 16:13-19

Real protection begins by knowing Jesus Christ as your Lord and Savior, just like Peter knew Him in this passage of Scripture. If your kids are not saved, this is where you begin! Pray that everywhere they go and everyone they meet will tell them about Jesus in some way, that the Holy Spirit will convict them and bring them into the body of Christ.

Jesus told Peter that because he knew and accepted who He was, Peter was blessed. Furthermore, the gates of hell would not prevail against Peter or anyone who believed on Jesus in the same way. That's why I say that your kids' protection begins with knowing Jesus as "the Christ, the Son of the living God." Just being members of the body of Christ places your kids under God's sovereign, supernatural protection.

Jesus went on to say that not only would the gates of hell not prevail against those who believed in Him, but He also gave them the keys to the kingdom of God. Whatever they bound on earth in prayer would be bound in heaven, and whatever they loosed on earth in prayer would be loosed in heaven. Your prayers influence what your kids' experience will be with regard to heaven and earth. Whatever you pray over them affects their world and influences the decisions they make.

Therefore, the first step in seeing that your child is protected by God is to pray for them to be born again and part of the family of God. If they are already saved, then you can confidently pray God's Word over them.

Praying God's Word

In the beginning of this book I said that I like to see results when I pray, which is why I like to pray

God's Word. When I pray God's Word over kids, I know I am praying God's perfect will for them; and if I am praying God's perfect will, then I know my prayers will be answered. By praying His Word, I'm in agreement with Him about His will for the kids I am praying for.

One of the best passages of Scripture to pray over the kids in your life regarding protection is Psalm 91. This psalm is wonderful because it contains specific guidelines for how we can pray, and it covers every problem a human being can encounter in life. I encourage you to read it, study it, memorize it, and pray it every day. Here are a few key verses.

> He who dwells in the secret place of the Most High shall abide under the shadow of the Almighty.
> I will say of the LORD, "He is my refuge and my fortress; My God, in Him I will trust."
> Surely He shall deliver you from the snare of the fowler And from the perilous pestilence.
> He shall cover you with His feathers, And under His wings you shall take refuge; His truth shall be your shield and buckler.
> You shall not be afraid of the terror by night, Nor of the arrow that flies by day,

Nor of the pestilence that walks in darkness, Nor of the destruction that lays waste at noonday.

A thousand may fall at your side, And ten thousand at your right hand; But it shall not come near you.

Psalm 91:1-7

We won't discuss every verse, but we will look at the verses that touch on the key areas where Satan can try to come in and hurt or kill our kids. However, first I want to give you a point of reference. Verse 2 says, "I will say of the Lord, 'He is my refuge and my fortress.'" Literally, the psalmist is declaring that he lives inside God. God is his strength, refuge, and military fortress.

A fortress is a place of protection from enemies, so living in God is the place of safety from all the attacks of the devil. We can pray, "God, You are the fortress of my children. You are their covering and their shelter. You are their protector." The psalmist goes on to say that God will deliver him from a number of things.

Verse 3: Snare of the Fowler

What is the snare of the fowler? A snare is an unseen trap of temptation or destruction that is set by the fowler, who is the devil and his demons. This is a trap that you cannot see unless God makes you aware of it, because He sees everything.

As our kids go out into the world, the devil will set traps for them. We can pray for God to deliver them from these unseen snares, and then the Holy Spirit will either show them the trap and how to avoid it or give them the plan to walk through it without being hurt. He can also change their direction so that they never go near the trap that was set for them or have any knowledge that it ever existed!

Verse 3: Perilous Pestilence

"Perilous pestilence" is an infection, disease, or sickness. Thank God that He can deliver our kids and keep them from physical illness. Along with this verse in Psalm 91, we can also pray these verses for our kids' health and well being.

> Himself bore our sins in His own body on the tree, that we, having died to sins, might live for righteousness—by whose stripes you were healed.
>
> 2 Peter 2:24

He sent His word and healed them, And delivered them from their destructions.

Psalm 107:20

Verse 5: Terror by Night

God will see to it that our kids will not be afraid of the terror by night. The terror by night encompasses all the fears that can attack them when it is dark. This includes terrible dreams and nightmares, "seeing" bears and bad guys in the bedroom, or imagining there are monsters under their beds.

A burglar is another terror by night. A storm, a tornado, or a hurricane can be a terror by night. Anything that brings fear through darkness is a terror by night. You can stop those fears from coming to your kids by praying God's Word over them.

Verse 5: Arrows by Day

In the Bible an arrow sometimes refers to human beings. Psalm 127:4 says, "As arrows are in the hand of a mighty man; so are children of the youth." When we pray for our kids and train them up to love and serve God, they are like arrows that He can shoot to hit the target He is wanting to hit. But in Psalm 91:5

we read about "the arrow that flies by day." This is not a good arrow, but instead it is someone or something that is sent by the enemy to hurt and even destroy our kids.

There may be a teacher or a coach in their school who has it out for them. Someone they think is a friend might be winning their trust to try to introduce them to drugs or sex. The school curriculum may include a course that subtly undermines the truths that the Bible teaches, or a wolf can even creep into their youth group or children's church to try to deceive them and draw them away from you, the church, and God.

Whatever or whoever that arrow is, Psalm 91 says that God will protect kids from those arrows that come in the daytime to harm or damage them. Psalm 91 says you can pray this in confidence!

Verse 6: Pestilence That Walks in Darkness

Darkness is always associated with evil in the Bible. So "pestilence that walks in darkness" is a sickness that works in dark places, that is associated with evil, ungodly thinking and wicked behavior. Some of the things we would classify as "pestilence that walks in darkness" would be all kinds of addictions, such as drugs, alcohol, gluttony or food addictions, sexual promiscuity, and sexually transmitted diseases. It also includes those who are in bondage to things like anorexia and bulimia. God gives us His Word in Psalm 91 that He delivers them out of all of them!

Verse 6: Destruction at Noonday

"Destruction at noonday is any kind of calamity or accident, such as a car accident, mishap on the playground, or getting injured in a sports event. But in verse 7 God's Word says that a thousand may fall on one side of our kids and ten thousand on the other side, but God will protect them right where they stand.

It doesn't matter what the newspapers are saying, what statistics the experts cite, or that your father died from a terrible accident at age forty and so did your grandfather. These things did not matter the moment you were born again into God's kingdom. In His kingdom you are under His protection—and so are your kids!

When your kids get old enough to drive, you really want to begin to pray for them! At this writing, Cathy and I have two kids who have cars. When each of them got their car, the first thing we did was pray over them and their car. We prayed for protection, for the cars to work perfectly, and for them to drive wisely and safely. We prayed that they would not be harmed by another driver, but also that they would not harm anyone else.

Can I tell you that nothing has ever happened to our kids because we prayed? No. But I can tell you about God's supernatural protection in the midst of the "destruction at noonday." Just after he got his driver's license, my oldest son pulled out to cross a very busy highway. It was raining, and just as he entered that dangerous intersection, his tire exploded. He hit the gas to try to make it across the highway, and the car turned and spun around. In seconds the car stopped spinning and came to a halt right at the side of the road, completely out of harm's way!

My second son also had a car accident about two months after he had started driving. His car was totaled. When I went to look at it, it was mangled and an absolute mess. I was shocked because when my son had come home, he didn't even have a scratch on him! He had worn his seatbelt, but more important, he had had our prayers for God's protection.

Stuff Happens

In our world things are going to happen. If you think that your kid is never going to fall down, be attacked by sickness, or have any kind of problem, you're wrong. However, no matter what happens, God is going to be there to protect them as you pray and believe Him for their safety, success, and well being.

In Acts, chapter 27, Paul and two hundred other men and women were on a ship when the weather turned ugly and the ship sank. God's man, the great and powerful apostle Paul, was on board, and still the ship went down!

How would the body of Christ react if a great man of God, who was known for signs and wonders and miracles in his ministry, was flying to minister some-where, and his airplane crashed? Even if he and the other passengers were uninjured, there would be all kinds of discussion about why this happened. Was this an attack of the enemy? Was he in sin? Did he get out of God's will? Was he ignoring the Holy Spirit?

We can learn a lot from the apostle Paul's case in Acts, chapter 17. He had warned the sailors that they should not sail, but they ignored him. Then, when the storm struck, he had prayed and God had told him that although the ship and all its cargo would be lost, everyone on board the ship would live.

God also told Paul the reason he and the others were being spared: Paul had to fulfill God's will for his life and be brought before Caesar to testify of Jesus. There was supernatural protection in that calamity because Paul was a man of prayer and he was in the will of God. Therefore, we must pray for our kids to know God's will and do it, because that is a place of safety.

As for Paul, after the ship had run aground on the island and all the people were safe, he helped build a fire and was attacked again. In Acts 28:3-5 a snake "fastened on his hand." But he shook it off and the venom had no effect on him. God could have prevented the snake, but He didn't because Paul's deliverance was a witness of God's power to the islanders.

Prayer doesn't *eliminate* the problems of life for our kids; prayer moves God to *deliver them* from the problems of life. Even when negative and catastrophic things happen, He will be supernaturally there to protect them, to perform His will, to give them His wisdom, to empower them, and to care for them.

Sometimes we think it is God's best to avoid all problems in life, but that just doesn't happen on planet earth today! That's why I love what it says in Psalm 34:19, "Many are the afflictions of the righteous, but the Lord delivers him out of them all."

Prayer for Protection

Father, in the name of Jesus, we thank You for our kids, and we pray that You would be their refuge and fortress, that their protection would be in You. We pray that no evil will come upon them. Neither will any sickness, evil, or calamity come near their dwelling. Thank You for commissioning Your angels to guard, to protect, and to defend them from all harm. We pray that no weapon that is designed against them will succeed, and every tongue that would rise up against them will be silenced. Great will be their peace and undisturbed composure because their righteousness is from You. We thank You for Your delivering hand of protection in whatever challenge or attack they face. In the name of Jesus we pray, amen.

3

Favor of God

But let all those rejoice who put their trust in You; Let them ever shout for joy, because You defend them; Let those also who love Your name be joyful in You.

For You, O Lord, will bless the righteous; With favor You will surround him as with a shield.

Psalm 5:11,12

As we teach our kids to trust God, that He protects them and defends them, we can also pray confidently that He surrounds them with His favor wherever they go. We call it the F-O-G, Favor Of God. We must pray for kids to walk in the FOG! The world uses the term "walking in a fog" as a negative thing, but believers can have a different perception because they walk in God's light.

Fog in the natural is an interesting phenomenon because it reflects light. Darkness is completely expelled by light, and the Bible says that it cannot comprehend light. But fog reflects light. For example, when you learn to drive you are taught to turn your headlights on dim if it is foggy; otherwise, the reflection of the headlights from the fog can blind your vision. In essence, FOG multiplies light.

The FOG, or favor of God, is intimately connected to light. The two go hand in hand. For example, when a kid is filled with the Spirit and walks into the room, it seems like the whole room lights up. You just want to jump up and find some way to bless them. That's God's favor. When the light of the Spirit is flowing out of them, the favor of God is all over them.

We can pray that our kids will reflect the light of Jesus Christ wherever they go and whatever they do, because when they reflect Him they have favor with God and man. Jesus told us that we are "the light of the world."

> You are the light of the world. A city that is set on a hill cannot be hidden.
>
> Nor do they light a lamp and put it under a basket, but on a lampstand, and it gives light to all who are in the house.

Let your light so shine before men, that they may see
your good works and glorify your Father in heaven.

Matthew 5:14-16

When our kids go out into the world to school, to
work, or to play, we should pray that they will let their
light shine and act like Jesus. Then, as they reflect His
light, they also will be walking in His favor.

When Moses led the children of Israel out of
Egypt, God gave him a prayer of blessing to pray
over His people. This prayer of blessing tells us that
God's light and favor go together.

And the Lord spoke to Moses, saying:
"Speak to Aaron and his sons, saying, "This is
the way you shall bless the children of Israel. Say
to them:
"The Lord bless you and keep you;
The Lord make His face shine upon you, And be
gracious to you;
The Lord lift up His countenance upon you, And
give you peace.""

Numbers 6:22-26

Walking in God's favor means His face is shining
upon us! This blessing truly reveals the love that God
has for His children and how He favors us and gives

us favor with others. He wants us to be blessed, protected, and given special treatment in this world. Because He is the only one who can make these things happen, He instructed Moses to pray that He would bless the children of Israel. We can pray this same blessing over our kids.

When we pray for our children to be blessed of the Lord, we can pray for His face to shine upon them, that He will be gracious to them and give them peace. And the Hebrew words for "lift" and "countenance" in verse 26 are very interesting. The Hebrew word for "lift" can mean many things, including "accept, advance,…forgive,…give,…help,…honourable,…marry,…respect."[1]

The Hebrew word for "countenance" also has many possible meanings, including "enquire,… face,…and favour." But the main idea is "the face (as the part that turns)."[2] The Hebrew language is painting a picture of the Lord turning His face to His kids to hear what they have to say and to accept them, advance them, forgive them, give to them, help them, honor them, be married to them in spiritual intimacy, and respect them. In other words, He favors His kids because His kids are His favorites! Whenever our kids call upon His name,

He immediately turns to give them His full attention and bless them in that situation.

God's Kids Have Favor!

God wants to surround His kids with supernatural favor just like a shield. This means that everywhere His kids go they will have good will, partiality, special treatment, and extra support to make life easier and to be able to do what God has called them to do. In the Bible, we can see that many of the Old Testament saints prayed for favor with other people. Ruth prayed for favor with Boaz in Ruth 2:13. David prayed for favor in Psalm 119:58. They knew only God could grant them favor, especially with their enemies.

When Jacob returned home years after he had treacherously stolen the first son's birthright from his brother Esau, he was afraid Esau would try to kill him. In Genesis 32:5 he sent messengers ahead to announce his coming, saying, "I have sent to tell my lord, that I may find favor in your sight." He asked Esau for favor, and in this case that meant mercy and forgiveness.

The messengers returned to tell Jacob that Esau was coming out to meet him with four hundred men, so Jacob hit his knees and prayed for God to deliver him.

Then Jacob said, "O God of my father Abraham and God of my father Isaac,....

Deliver me, I pray, from the hand of my brother, from the hand of Esau; for I fear him, lest he come and attack me and the mother with the children.

For You said, "I will surely treat you well, and make your descendants as the sand of the sea, which cannot be numbered for multitude."

Genesis 32:9,11,12

Jacob reminded God of the favor He had promised him! As a result, his meeting with Esau was peaceful and joyous.

Then he [Jacob] crossed over before them and bowed himself to the ground seven times, until he came near to his brother.

But Esau ran to meet him, and embraced him, and fell on his neck and kissed him, and they wept.

Genesis 33:3,4 [insert mine]

This is great favor! Jacob faced a terrible situation. He knew that his brother Esau was a wild man and that there was a good chance Esau hated Jacob for stealing the birthright and then skipping town. But God gave Jacob such supernatural favor that Esau ran to meet him, hugged him, kissed him, and wept with joy to see him.

Just like Jacob, we can remind God that He has promised our kids favor with both friends and enemies when we pray for them. And also just like Jacob, no matter how difficult the situation, we can expect and have faith that God's favor will deliver them from all harm.

Increasing in Favor

In the New Testament, we know that Jesus was born with the favor of God but increased in it as He grew older. In the gospel of Luke, speaking of Jesus as a young boy, the Bible says, "And Jesus increased in wisdom and stature, and in favor with God and men." The very early church of Acts enjoyed incredible favor with the people in their day, and the Bible doesn't mention that they prayed for it. They just had it.

> Continuing daily with one accord in the temple, and breaking bread from house to house, they ate their food with gladness and simplicity of heart, praising God and having favor with all the people.
>
> Acts 2:46,47

From these verses of Scripture, it would seem that when we are born again we have the favor of God on us. Our kids need to understand that they are God's kids and His favor is on them. He loves them and wants to bless them. But even Jesus increased in favor, and we are to be like Him. We need to pray for the favor of God to be on our kids and for it to increase every day as they love Him and serve Him.

Favor in Action

I want to tell you the story of a girl that you may have heard of or read about. When she was in high school, she opened her yearbook and read these stinging words beneath her name and her picture: "Voted least likely to succeed." She didn't know that they were going to put that caption under her picture. It was a devastating shock to her young heart, but unfortunately not a new experience. From the fifth grade, this girl had been in a class for slow learners. Kids teased her and called her "dumb girl." They also nicknamed her "S-P-E-D" because she was always enrolled in special education classes.

She loved to play basketball, but she sat on the bench most of the time at games because she was so nervous and was terrified of messing up. Every time she got the ball, she would make a mistake and the coach would take her out. Her teammates called her "Retard."

Finally, as she stared at her yearbook that day, she was giving serious thought to suicide. She was fifteen years old, and it was the end of the school year. Thank God, during that time two people were there to help her get through that trying time. Her mother had suddenly become very serious about investing in her daughter's life and began to pray fervently for her. She may not have known that her daughter was contemplating suicide, but the Holy Spirit did. So He led her to pray, believe God, and speak God's Word over her daughter.

This girl also had a cousin who was a Christian, and the Holy Spirit tapped her on the shoulder, too. She not only prayed for her, but she sent her Christian tapes and books and encouraged her to believe what God said about her instead of all the lies she had heard at school—and read in her yearbook.

That summer this young woman decided to change her self-image. She chose to believe what the Bible said about her. She began to realize that God believed in her, that He loved her, that He favored her, and that He cared about her. Slowly but surely, she began to change the way she thought about herself. Instead of looking at herself in the mirror and seeing a loser, a retard, or "SPED;" she began to call herself, "victorious," "a champion," and "highly favored of God."

The next basketball season she came off the bench and began to play better than she had ever played before. By the end of the year her team voted her the most valuable player on the team. She began to apply herself in class with a new confidence and desire to succeed, and her teachers were amazed. Her grades went up, and she was moved out of special education classes into regular classes.

Today this woman preaches on television and radio. She speaks to huge crowds in some of the largest auditoriums around the world and tells them how God delivered her and gave her favor. Her name is Kate McVeigh, and she wrote an incredible book on the favor of God called, *The Blessing of Favor!*[3]

The question I must put to you is, *What would have happened if Kate's mother and cousin had not prayed for her?*

There is something extremely important to learn from this story. When the Holy Spirit brings a kid to mind or puts them on our hearts, whether it is our kid or someone else's kid, we need to pray for them. We may not know what is happening to them or what they are going through, so we need to pray for them to have the favor of God and increase in the favor of God every day.

No matter where your kids are right now, as you begin to pray for the favor of God to be upon them, believe and expect that changes can and will happen, just like they did for Kate.

Prayer for Favor

Father, in the name of Jesus we believe that our children are blessed of You, that they are surrounded with Your favor as a shield. We believe that Your face shines upon them, that You are gracious to them in all circumstances. We thank You for turning Your face to them whenever they call Your name, that they have Your full attention and assistance in all situations. We pray that throughout the day people in their lives will be predisposed to want to bless and encourage them. We pray that they will enjoy unusual cooperation and overwhelming goodwill in all their activities. We thank You that they will walk in favor with You, shining the light of the gospel into others' lives, and therefore be complemented with favor and promotion from others. In Jesus' name we pray, amen.

4

Boldness

And take the helmet of salvation, and the sword of the Spirit, which is the word of God;

praying always with all prayer and supplication in the Spirit, being watchful to this end with all perseverance and supplication for all the saints—

and for me, that utterance may be given to me, that I may open my mouth boldly to make known the mystery of the gospel,

for which I am an ambassador in chains; that in it I may speak boldly, as I ought to speak.

Ephesians 6:17-20

This is a very familiar passage of Scripture, beginning with the last part of the armor of God in Ephesians, chapter 6. But then in verses 19 and 20 Paul went on to ask the church at Ephesus to pray for him, that he would preach the gospel boldly. If Paul, the great apostle, needed to ask other believers to pray for him to have boldness in his calling, then we should have no hesitation in praying for each other to have boldness as we serve the Lord—and that includes the kids in our lives!

Paul had learned that without the power of the Holy Spirit, nothing was going to happen in his ministry.

> And my speech and my preaching were not with persuasive words of human wisdom, but in demonstration of the Spirit and of power,
>
> that your faith should not be in the wisdom of men but in the power of God.
>
> 1 Corinthians 2:4,5

Demonstration of the Spirit and of power requires a boldness to obey the Spirit and move in His power. As one of the great missionaries and apostles of his day, Paul realized that he needed the anointing of the Holy Spirit to be bold, that he could not rely on his own strength or wisdom. We need to pray for our kids to have that same boldness, which means we need to teach them the vital role of the Holy Spirit in their lives.

> For God did not give us a spirit of timidity (of cowardice, of craven and cringing and fawning fear), but [He has given us a spirit] of power and of love

and of calm and well-balanced mind and discipline
and self-control.

2 Timothy 1:7 AMP

Without the power of the Holy Spirit in their lives,
our kids can be easily intimidated by those who
oppose the gospel, and they can actually be afraid of
sharing Jesus with people who are lost. They can fear
everything from simple rejection to blatant persecu-
tion, especially from their friends and acquaintances
at school. To defeat all fear and have a holy boldness,
kids need the baptism of the Holy Ghost.

The Baptism of the Holy Ghost

We must be faithful to teach kids about the
baptism of the Holy Spirit, especially if we are
leading them to the Lord. Remember, Jesus told His
disciples not to go anywhere or to do anything until
they were baptized with the Holy Ghost.

And being assembled together with them, He com-
manded them not to depart from Jerusalem, but to
wait for the Promise of the Father, "which," He
said, "you have heard from Me;

for John truly baptized with water, but you shall be baptized with the Holy Spirit not many days from now."

But you shall receive power when the Holy Spirit has come upon you; and you shall be witnesses to Me in Jerusalem, and in all Judea and Samaria, and to the end of the earth."

Acts 1:4-5,8

Our kids need to understand that Jesus is the same yesterday, today, and forever (see Hebrews 13:8). He saves and baptizes in the Holy Ghost today just as He baptized His first disciples in the Holy Ghost in Jerusalem.

When the Day of Pentecost had fully come, they were all with one accord in one place.

And suddenly there came a sound from heaven, as of a rushing mighty wind, and it filled the whole house where they were sitting.

Then there appeared to them divided tongues, as of fire, and one sat upon each of them.

And they were all filled with the Holy Spirit and began to speak with other tongues, as the Spirit gave them utterance.

Acts 2:1-4

There may or may not be tongues of fire when Jesus baptizes them in the Holy Ghost, but there will definitely be tongues! And they will receive power to be witnesses for Jesus in their world, to share their faith and live godly lives, showing people God's goodness wherever they go. Being filled with the Holy Spirit gives all believers—including kids—boldness to tell the gospel story and live godly lives.

Speaking in tongues is more than a supernatural experience or "spiritual high." It is also a vehicle God uses to get us where He needs us to go and do what He has called us to do. As we pray in the Spirit, we are filled with His power and our faith increases.

> But you, beloved, building yourselves up on your most holy faith, praying in the Holy Spirit,....
>
> Jude 1:20

Praying in tongues builds up our faith, and kids need great faith to be bold witnesses for Jesus Christ in the world they live in today. They need to be filled and stay filled with the power of the Holy Spirit so they can be bold, strong, and confident in serving the Lord. To stay filled, we need to pray that they speak in tongues whenever they can.

This prompts me to ask you a question. How much do *you* speak in tongues? Paul said in 1 Corinthians 14:18 that he spoke with tongues more than anyone he knew. In 1 Thessalonians 5:17 he told us to never stop praying, and in Colossians 1:9 he told the Colossians that he never stopped praying for them. That's a lot of praying!

Have you ever tried to pray continuously, all day long? There is absolutely no way you can pray all day without either being silent for long lengths of time (which is good if you are listening to the Holy Spirit) or praying in tongues. The beauty of praying in tongues is that the Bible says you are praying mysteries to God (1 Corinthians 14:2) that you do not understand unless the Holy Spirit gives you the interpretation.

It is possible to pray in tongues when your mind doesn't know what else to pray. Romans 8:26-27 tells us that the Holy Spirit will intercede for others as He gives us the utterance in tongues. And while we are praying in tongues, our faith is being built up to be bold witnesses for God.

The point I am making is that we should be an example to our kids by praying in tongues as much as possible. Then we can encourage them to do the

same. Praying in the Spirit increases faith and boldness to witness for the Lord Jesus Christ. And when
the Holy Ghost fills kids to overflowing, His love
captures their hearts and eradicates any fear they have
of telling others about the Lord. God's love is the
power that transforms us from chickens to lions!

Transforming Love

> Love has been perfected among us in this: that we
> may have boldness in the day of judgment; because
> as He is, so are we in this world.
> There is no fear in love; but perfect love casts
> out fear.
>
> 1 John 4:17,18

Where does the rubber meet the road in life? What
is the moment in time that determines our eternal
state and dwelling place, the moment when no human
being will have any excuse for their bad behavior?
That is the day of judgment, the day when every
person who has ever lived will stand before God and
be judged for their life on earth.

As believers, we have boldness to approach that
day confidently because Jesus Christ has wiped away
our debt of sin. God has nothing against us and we

are His beloved children. Therefore, we have nothing to fear because of His love for us. His perfect love casts out all fear—of judgment and of anything that can happen to us in this life. We are His children, He loves us, and His love for us destroys any fear that comes against us.

In the same way that our Father's love has transformed our lives, His love also transforms our kids' lives—directly or indirectly through us and others. His love flowing through us to our kids transforms their lives, giving them confidence and driving out every fear. They are built up and encouraged just knowing that we are praying for them, believing the best for them, and love them in spite of their faults and weaknesses. Love inspires boldness.

Our love for our kids causes us to desire the very best for them in every area of their lives. Love drives out all fear when our kids act weird or don't meet our expectations. And love is what motivates us to pray and believe God even in the most trying circumstances, when our kids or the kids in our lives seem to be stuck in a rut. Cathy and I faced such a situation with our middle son, Dillon.

Boldness

When Dillon was very young, he was tremendously insecure. He was afraid of everybody. When we would visit friends or relatives, he would just stand in the shadows or hide behind Cathy or me. We would try to get him to introduce himself and talk to people, but he wouldn't do it.

We'd say, "Now come on, go ahead and say hello."

And he'd say, "Hmmm, I don't want to do it." He was one of the shyest little kids we had ever known.

So Cathy and I began to pray, "Lord, we just pray that You will give Dillon boldness. We pray that You will cause him to engage socially, to be friendly, and to meet people. We ask You to help him develop personality and come out of himself, to work well with people, and that he will be a friend to other kids."

Today Dillon is one of the friendliest young men you'll ever meet. As the saying goes, he has never met a stranger. Every person is his friend. He will go out of his way to make you feel welcome and comfortable. But those of us who were around when he was little know that his behavior now is a miracle from God! Dillon's boldness is the Spirit of God working in him.

Let's pray now for our kids to have that same boldness.

Prayer for Boldness

Father, in the name of Jesus we pray that You will give each one of our kids a spirit of boldness as they walk with You. We pray that the power of the Holy Spirit will rise up within them to be witnesses for Jesus Christ in all they do. We pray that they will never be ashamed of the gospel, but they will realize it is Your power working in their salvation, as well as the salvation of hurting people. We thank You that they don't operate with fear, intimidation, or appre-hension. Instead, they are as bold as lions, possessing strength, confidence, and steadfast minds and hearts. We thank You, Father, for Your love toward us and our kids, that Your love never fails, and that Your love transforms our kids into powerful, bold witnesses for Jesus Christ and Your kingdom. In the name of Jesus we pray, amen.

5

Find and Fulfill Their
God-Given Assignment

A man's gift makes room for him, And brings him
before great men.

Proverbs 18:16

It's God's will for kids to find and fulfill the
assignment He has for them. As adults, we need to
identify and develop the gifts of God in our kids and
the kids in our lives that we influence and impact.
Each child possesses something unique and special,
something in their life in which they are highly
skilled, and we need to pray that their assignment
regarding their gifts comes forth and is fully realized.

Over the years I have learned that you can predict
the future of a teenager by their awareness of their
assignment from God. I have done this just by talking
with them for a few minutes. I find out what they like

to do, what they are interested in, what their plans are, and what goals they have set for themselves. How much they have thought about these issues and what they have decided about them determines their immediate future.

With that in mind, we need to pray for kids to be aware that God has assignments for their lives, and these assignments are connected with the way God has gifted them, with the abilities and talents that they have. We need to engage our kids in praying about their future, the call of God on their life, how they will support themselves in a profession, what their ministry is (if it is different from the career they are called to pursue), and the steps that they are going to take to realize their dreams.

Kids are never too young to begin thinking about these things because it gives them a righteous sense of purpose, that God created them for a reason. They will walk in the confidence that they are a significant part of His plan and are valuable and precious to Him.

Jeremiah's Call

Jeremiah was a very young man when God called him and set him apart to serve Him as a prophet. When we read the account in the Bible, it is evident that Jeremiah was pretty unnerved by the whole thing. But God talked to him and tried to put his heart at ease. When we pray for our kids to hear from God regarding their assignments in life, we also need to pray for God to give them peace and confidence about their call. Like Jeremiah, we want them to know in their innermost being that God is with them, He will always be with them, and they don't need to be afraid of anything or anybody.

> Then the word of the LORD came to me, saying:
>
> "Before I formed you in the womb I knew you; Before you were born I sanctified you; I ordained you a prophet to the nations."
>
> Then said I: "Ah, Lord God! Behold, I cannot speak, for I am a youth."
>
> But the Lord said to me: "Do not say, "I am a youth,' For you shall go to all to whom I send you, And whatever I command you, you shall speak.
>
> Do not be afraid of their faces, For I am with you to deliver you," says the Lord.
>
> Jeremiah 1:4-8

God told Jeremiah that before he was even conceived, He knew him and ordained him to be a prophet to the nations. And when Jeremiah protested that he was too young, God instructed him not to talk about how young he was with Him or anyone else. God was not interested in Jeremiah's age; He was interested in seeing him discover and then carry out the assignment He gave him. God is still not interested in age, and He still wants to see young people find out and then accomplish His will for their lives.

God prepared Jeremiah at a very young age, and He wants to prepare our kids today as early as possible. Kids are never too young for God to speak to them. He told Jeremiah, "I've called you. I've anointed you, and don't give me excuses about why you can't do it or how you're too young. You're going to go where I called you to go. You're going to speak what I tell you to speak. And you're going to be a prophet to the nations."

Hell's greatest fear is a child's discovery of and passion to fulfill their God-given gifts and assignments. The devil doesn't want a kid to know what God's plans are for them and will do anything he can to keep them from seeing God's truth about themselves. That's why we need to pray for them and with them about their future. We need to pray for them to hear what God is saying to them about their gifts and callings. And we need to ask them what God is doing in their lives, what dreams He has placed in their hearts, and what steps they see themselves taking to fulfill those dreams.

The sooner we begin talking to kids about these issues, the sooner they will begin seeking God for their assignments and stepping out to fulfill them. And the sooner they begin seeking God for their assignments and taking steps to fulfill them, the less likely the devil will be able to stop them!

Passion Anchors the Soul

There is nothing more powerful in a young person's life than having a passion for what God has called them to do. This passion keeps them anchored in and focused on godly pursuits, and they are less vulnerable to the temptations and distractions of the enemy. From the time God spoke to Jeremiah, every day he woke up with a sense of purpose and meaning to his life. I would venture to say that he didn't even think about getting into drugs or crime because he was too busy pursuing the call of God on his life. We need to pray for our kids to have that same Holy Ghost revelation and fire regarding God's will for their lives.

My life has been incredibly influenced by the prayers of my mother. She prayed for me to love and serve

God, to know what He was calling me to do and to do it. When I was eighteen we went on a camping trip, and during that vacation I saw myself reaching the next generation like Oral Roberts reached his generation.

This vision and dream gave me a focus for my life and resulted in the television show *Fire by Night* and one of the biggest youth gatherings for God in the United States, Oneighty, both which were produced under the leadership of Pastor Willie George, my pastor and mentor. Pastor George has had a similar call to reach kids for Jesus Christ, and he has encouraged me and prayed for me to keep my passion to reach my generation.

My mother's prayers and the prayers of countless others like Pastor George have had a supernatural impact on my life, and then my life has had a spiritual impact on countless kids who have watched *Fire by Night* or have attended Oneighty. I have had numerous opportunities to pray for and with kids, and have seen firsthand how their lives are radically changed when they find and then pursue God's plan for their lives.

God Empowers and Instructs

When God called Jeremiah to be a prophet to the nations, He also empowered him to do what He was calling him to do and instructed him in exactly how he was going to operate as a prophet.

> Then the Lord put forth His hand and touched my mouth, and the Lord said to me: "Behold, I have put My words in your mouth.
> See, I have this day set you over the nations and over the kingdoms, To root out and to pull down, To destroy and to throw down, To build and to plant."
>
> Jeremiah 1:9,10

When we talk to kids about their calling we need to show them these verses of Scripture. We need to pray for them to be empowered and strengthened by God to do what He's calling them to do. God first touched Jeremiah's mouth because Jeremiah was going to speak for Him. He anointed Jeremiah's mouth to be His instrument of ministry to the people.

We need to pray that our kids will hear God's specific instructions, so there is no confusion about the next step they are to take. God told Jeremiah that He was setting him in authority "over the nations and over the kingdoms." That was a lot of territory! No wonder Jeremiah was nervous about being young. But God assured him that He would help him do great exploits.

God also told Jeremiah what he was going to be doing in the authority He was giving him. He would root out, pull down, destroy and throw down, to build and to plant. That's a lot of action for a young kid! Again, we can understand why Jeremiah was overwhelmed. His assignment was to destroy the works of unrighteousness and then build and plant God's works of righteousness.

When our kids begin to see what God has assigned them to do, it can be overwhelming as well as exciting. We must pray for them to be fully empowered and strengthened, to feel and hear the encouragement and instruction of the Holy Spirit just as Jeremiah did. We must pray for them to hear those specific instructions and to courageously obey them.

Motivate, Don't Pressure

As you notice a kid's attributes, qualities, gifts, and talents, don't put pressure on them. Motivate them. Challenge them. Inspire them. Encourage them. You can ask them questions that will cause them to think and pray about what God's purpose for their life is. You can make suggestions and offer opportunities to develop their gifts and callings.

Motivate them to explore, experiment with, and discover what God has for them. You might not know exactly where they are going or what they are going to do, but you can help them in their process of hearing from God and carrying out His will for their lives. You want the kids in your life to be arrows that are skillfully launched and hit their targets. And the most important thing you can do for them is pray!

Prayer To Fulfill Their Assignment

Father, we thank You for blessing our kids and empowering them to do the right things, to find their gifts and assignments from heaven. We pray that the unique abilities You have placed in them will make room for them and bring them before the great leaders of our day. We pray that they will walk in accuracy and obedience to accomplish Your perfect will for their lives. We know that You have given them a holy and distinct calling, and that You will reveal the specific steps they are to take in fulfilling that call. Help them to faithfully develop their talents and their gifts in such a way that will place them in high regard and great demand in this world. In Jesus' name we pray, amen.

6

Find the Right Mate

It is never too early to start praying for kids to marry the right person. God wants your son to find the right wife and your daughter to find the right husband. He wants the boys and girls in your life to grow up and marry according to His will. After receiving Jesus Christ as their Lord and Savior, whom they marry is the second most important decision they will make in life. If they marry the right person, it can do wonders; but if they marry the wrong person, their lives can be filled with trouble and misery.

Biblical Examples

The Bible gives us clear examples of good marriages and bad marriages and how they affected believers. One of the examples of a bad marriage was when Samson married a Philistine girl.

Find the Right Mate

Now Samson went down to Timnah, and saw a woman in Timnah of the daughters of the Philistines.

So he went up and told his father and mother, saying, "I have seen a woman in Timnah of the daughters of the Philistines; now therefore, get her for me as a wife."

Then his father and mother said to him, "Is there no woman among the daughters of your brethren, or among all my people, that you must go and get a wife from the uncircumcised Philistines?" And Samson said to his father, "Get her for me, for she pleases me well."

Judges 14:1-3

In Deuteronomy 7:3 God forbid the Israelites to marry outside their nation, but throughout his life Samson married and had intimate relationships with women who were not from Israel. He first married a Philistine woman, and Scripture says that God used the trouble in that marriage for Samson to kill many Philistines. Later, Samson formed a liaison with Delilah, and God used that to destroy more Philistines. But how much more could Samson have accomplished if he had listened to his parents and married wisely?

An example of a great marriage is Aquila and Priscilla in the book of Acts. They were Jewish tentmakers like Paul and befriended him when he came to Corinth. Together they made tents, preached and taught God's Word, and even traveled to other cities to spread the gospel. They were a tremendous help to Paul and a powerful ministry team who taught other disciples and ministers such as Apollos.

> Now a certain Jew named Apollos, born at Alexandria, an eloquent man and mighty in the Scriptures, came to Ephesus.
>
> This man had been instructed in the way of the Lord; and being fervent in spirit, he spoke and taught accurately the things of the Lord, though he knew only the baptism of John.
>
> So he began to speak boldly in the synagogue. When Aquila and Priscilla heard him, they took him aside and explained to him the way of God more accurately.
>
> Acts 18:24-26

Aquila and Priscilla were a great example of how a husband and wife can serve the Lord together. It is good to teach kids about these good and bad examples from an early age, and then pray with them to be wise like Aquila and Priscilla so that they can serve God fully and powerfully.

Preparation Time

In Genesis 2:18 God declared that it wasn't good for the man to be alone, and then He made the woman. From the time kids are small we need to teach them that one day they will be married and that God says that marriage is a blessing. Why do I say that? Because in today's world, especially on television shows and even in kids' movies, marriage is often shown in a very negative way. We need to pray that the worldly concepts of the marriage relationship don't influence them, that only the Bible and godly examples of marriage will be their guide.

The Bible says that we are to train kids in all the ways of the Lord, and that includes marriage. We need to pray *for* them and *with* them concerning their mate and teach them what the Bible says about marriage. When they see how seriously God takes marriage, they will take it seriously too. And when they understand what a joy and blessing God created marriage to be, they will look forward to it.

God's Order

> But I want you to know that the head of every man
> is Christ, the head of woman is man, and the head
> of Christ is God.
>
> 1 Corinthians 11:3

We need to always pray for God's order to reign
in our kids' lives, and in this verse Paul reminds the
Corinthians of God's order in marriage. God is the
head of Jesus, Jesus is the head of the husband, and
the husband is the head of the woman. Paul is making
the point that even Jesus answers to someone, and we
all are in the middle of the submission and authority
structure in the body of Christ. We all are accountable
to someone over us and responsible for someone
under us.

It is very important for kids to know from the time
they are born that God loves and respects everyone
the same, but He places us in the body as He wills
(see 1 Corinthians 12:18). Part of that placement has
to do with marriage. Although boys and girls are equal
in God's eyes, He made them to function differently
in marriage. When we pray for kids regarding marriage, we need to pray according to God's Word. Then
they will be prepared for marriage when the right

person comes along. They will understand God's order and relate to their mate according to His Word.

Some verses of Scripture apply to both boys and girls, but many are for one or the other. Both should be taught that the Word of God has a lot to say about being a husband and being a wife, and they can learn to pray these Scriptures with you.

Parents First

Pray for your kids to honor you as their parents (or pray for the kids you know to honor their parents) because kids learn how they are to treat their future mate by honoring and submitting to their parents. Honoring their father and mother teaches them to honor and respect their future spouse. This idea also makes them set a godly standard for a mate. They realize that the husband or wife God will bring to them should be someone they can honor in the same way that they honor their parents, and someone who understands what it means to honor others.

> Children, obey your parents in the Lord, for this is right.
> "Honor your father and mother," which is the first commandment with promise:

"that it may be well with you and you may live long on the earth."

Ephesians 6:1-3

Obedience to parents reinforces God's order in a kid's life and reveals how God protects them as they submit to those in authority over them. And honoring their father and mother has a great promise that goes with it: they will live a long life and a good life. That includes the right mate and a godly marriage.

Boys

Husbands, likewise, dwell with them with understanding, giving honor to the wife, as to the weaker vessel, and as being heirs together of the grace of life, that your prayers may not be hindered.

1 Peter 3:7

This verse lets boys know that God was so concerned about how a husband treated his wife that He made it a standard to determine whether or not He would answer a husband's prayers! Young boys will probably gasp at this one, but then you can tell them that there is more for them to learn.

Husbands, love your wives, just as Christ also loved the church and gave Himself for her.

Ephesians 5:25

This verse tells them that they are to love their wives like Jesus loves the Church! When a boy realizes how he has to love, honor, respect, protect, and care for his future wife, he will gladly join in with your prayers that he marry the right one! He will not want to marry someone who is difficult to love, honor, respect, protect, and care for.

We must also pray that this boy will grow into the godly man he needs to be for his wife. Loving her as Jesus loves the Church is a tall order for even the strongest Christian man of God to fill, and so we must pray that he will draw close to God and grow strong in His wisdom, strength, and power. Again, when he recognizes the tremendous responsibility and honor God has given him in being a husband, he will be more likely to pray diligently and choose his wife prayerfully.

Together you can also pray that his future wife is growing up to love and obey God too, that God is preparing her to be a godly wife while He is preparing him to be a godly husband. He will want to marry someone who understands and respects his gifts and callings, who will encourage him as he fulfills God's will for his life. As you pray, believe that God is painting a picture in his heart of his future wife.

Then, when the time is right, he will recognize her and know that she is God's choice for him.

Girls

Most girls start thinking about getting married at an early age without any encouragement from adults. They play with dolls and imagine their own home and family, so we must pray that what they imagine is a godly picture and not a worldly one. We should teach them what God's Word says about being a wife and pray the Word over them and with them.

> Wives, submit to your own husbands, as to the Lord.
> For the husband is head of the wife, as also Christ is head of the church; and He is the Savior of the body.
> Therefore, just as the church is subject to Christ, so let the wives be to their own husbands in everything.
>
> Ephesians 5:22-24

When a little girl understands that she will submit to her husband just like she submits to Jesus, she will be more apt to join you in praying that she will marry the right man! Pray for her to marry a man who will not abuse his headship or lord it over her, but he will be a godly man who will love her, respect her, and cherish her. Pray for her to respect and honor him, and to understand that her influence on his life is very powerful and should not be abused either.

> In the same way, you wives must accept the authority of your husbands, even those who refuse to accept the Good News. Your godly lives will speak to them better than any words. They will be won over by watching your pure, godly behavior.
>
> Don't be concerned about the outward beauty that depends on fancy hairstyles, expensive jewelry, or beautiful clothes. You should be known for the beauty that comes from within, the unfading beauty of a gentle and quiet spirit, which is so precious to God.
>
> That is the way the holy women of old made themselves beautiful. They trusted God and accepted the authority of their husbands.
>
> 1 Peter 3:1-5 NLT

Praying these verses and teaching them to a young girl shapes and forms her perception of what a godly woman and wife is: how she should think, how she should look, and how she should behave. Pray that she will have a revelation at an early age that God is most interested in her heart, and that she should be waiting for a husband who will love her for who she is in Him and encourage her in her gifts and callings. At the same time, these verses challenge her to grow up to BE that woman! Pray that God will give her the grace to be that beautiful young woman with a gentle and quiet spirit, who obeys Him by doing His will for her life.

You will not only pray for her to wait for the right man, but many prayers will go up to heaven for that boy who will become her husband. You will want him to be a strong, godly man who knows his calling and purpose as well as his responsibility to love her, care for her, and inspire her to reach her full potential in God.

We must pray for boys and girls to see from God's Word what His design for marriage is and how a husband and wife are to think, act, and relate to one another. Above all, we must pray for them to understand and look for true love.

True Love

One of the great prayers you can pray for kids with regard to marriage is that they find true love with their husband or wife. God's most perfect definition of true love is found in 1 Corinthians 13, which we know as "the love chapter" of the Bible.

Love endures long and is patient and kind; love never is envious nor boils over with jealousy, is not boastful or vainglorious, does not display itself haughtily.

It is not conceited (arrogant and inflated with pride); it is not rude (unmannerly) and does not act unbecomingly. Love (God's love in us) does not insist on its own rights or its own way, for it is not self-seeking; it is not touchy or fretful or resentful; it takes no account of the evil done to it [it pays no attention to a suffered wrong].

It does not rejoice at injustice and unrighteousness, but rejoices when right and truth prevail.

Love bears up under anything and everything that comes, is ever ready to believe the best of every person, its hopes are fadeless under all circumstances, and it endures everything [without weakening].

Love never fails [never fades out or becomes obsolete or comes to an end].

1 Corinthians 13:4-8 AMP

This passage of Scripture describes what God's love is all about and how we are to love one another, particularly our mate. As you pray this passage over your kids, you can replace "love" with their name. You can pray, "[kid's name] endures long and is patient and kind." If the kid you are praying for is already married, you can pray "[kid's name and spouse's name] endure long and are patient and kind."

Romans 5:5 says that the love of God is shed abroad in our hearts by the Holy Spirit. As we pray for our kids to marry wisely and according to God's will, we know the Holy Spirit in them is causing God's love to flow in their hearts. Marriage is a partnership where a man and a woman become one in pursuing the call of God on their lives. The power behind their partnership is God's love and their love for one another.

Prayer for Future Mate

Father, in the name of Jesus, we pray for the right mate for each of our children and for the kids in our life, that they will marry in the right time and in the right way. We pray that You will cultivate and mature the love of God in their lives. Thank You for Your love, which abides and grows in their hearts by the Holy Ghost. We pray for that love to become apparent in their thoughts and actions daily. We pray that they will learn to esteem each other above themselves, to be composed, generous, truthful, and honorable in all they say and do. We thank You that they will be like Aquila and Priscilla, powerful partners in ministry. We pray that their courtship and engagement will be marked by poise and purity, and that their marriage will be tied and orchestrated in You. In Jesus' name we pray, amen.

7

Strength To Resist Temptation

Cathy gave me a book by Kenneth and Gloria Copeland, and they talked about a problem they had had with their son. He got into drugs and all kinds of messes, but today he is one of the key people on the staff of their ministry. He's serving God and he's strong in the Lord. How did his parents, these great ministers of the Word of God, pray for their son? They prayed a prayer from Jeremiah, chapter 31.

> Thus says the Lord: "Refrain your voice from weeping, And your eyes from tears; For your work shall be rewarded, says the Lord, And they shall come back from the land of the enemy.
>
> There is hope in your future, says the Lord, That your children shall come back to their own border.
>
> Jeremiah 31:16,17

They stood on these promises from God, trusting Him to bring their son back into fellowship with Him and His people, and He did. God will do the same for you if you take them to heart. Our temptation is to weep and worry for our kids and the kids we know who are in trouble, but God tells us to stop all negative emotion and to have faith that He will answer our prayers.

Before we go any further, if your son or daughter or a kid you know is not born again or serving the Lord, let's pray this prayer right now.

Father, in the mighty name of Jesus, we pray for [kid's name], who is out in the world and not serving You. We pray that You will bring them from the land of the enemy back into Your family. We thank You that we have the hope that their future is in You because You are bringing them into the borders of Your kingdom.

In the name of Jesus, we command Satan and all his demons to take their hands off of them, that the blinders will come off their eyes and they will see the truth of the Word of God. We pray for them to see the goodness of God unto salvation and pray for laborers to cross their path.

Thank You, Father, that they will see Jesus as their Savior and their Lord. They will know how much You

*love them, how good You are, and that You have a
great life for them. Through the eyes of faith we see
them saved, healed, delivered, and set free. We see
them loving You and serving You joyfully and faithfully in the body of Christ. We see them in church, and
we see them living a righteous life. We will not weep
or worry any longer because Your Word will not
come back void, but it will accomplish Your purpose
in their life. In Jesus' name we pray, amen.*

Influence Through Prayer

Our prayers do not supernaturally force our kids
to do everything we want them to do, but our prayers
go up to God and He can move on their hearts. We
cannot change the will of our kids; we can only influence them. Several months ago at church, a parent
came up for prayer. He said, "Pastor Blaine, can I
pray God's will to happen over my kids? Can I make
them do the right thing?"

Wouldn't that be nice? It would be great to be able
to pray, "In the name of Jesus, my kids will obey me
the rest of their lives. They will never have a rebellious attitude, they will never make a mistake or sin,
and they will never say or do anything wrong." That

would be wonderful! Unfortunately, we can't pray that way because they have a free will just like we have a free will. God doesn't force us into saying and doing things His way, and He won't force our kids either. However, the Holy Spirit is always speaking to us to influence us, and He can speak to our kids too.

You have great influence on the kids in your life, especially if they are living under your roof and therefore subject to your jurisdiction as a parent. You can give them guidance, correction, discipline, and wise counsel. When they rebel or make mistakes, you can bring them to an understanding of the blessings of God by grounding them or banning them from the phone and getting e-mail on the computer. When they obey, have a good attitude, and make right decisions, you can reward them with a slumber party or tickets to a skateboarding competition. There are all kinds of ways that you can influence their will toward godly thinking and behavior and encourage them to exercise good judgment while they are living in your home. And, of course, the most powerful influence (besides your prayers) is how you live your life before them. Your actions will always speak louder than your words!

Inevitably, however, there comes that time when they grow up, move away to college, get a job and their own apartment, and get married and establish their own home. If you are older and have children that are gone, you know that your influence begins to wane when they are no longer living in your home. You no longer have the physical jurisdiction, but you can still influence their decision-making with your prayers—and occasionally they may ask for your counsel.

We maintain influence over kids throughout their lives through our prayers. Even when they are young, they will be going to school, staying all night with friends, going to parties, and participating in many other activities that take them away from our over-sight. So begin praying for them when they are con-ceived! After all, we can't see them when they are in the womb, and we won't be seeing what they are doing and whom they are with for most of their lives. If they are the kids down the street or the kids in our Sunday school class, we will see them even less. We have precious few moments of face-to-face contact with kids, even when they are our own.

Prayer and faith in God to believe His best for their lives is always the greatest and most important thing we can do for any kid in this world. And there are some key verses of Scripture we should pray over them as they deal with the temptations of the enemy.

Love That Passes Knowledge

For this reason I bow my knees to the Father of our Lord Jesus Christ,

from whom the whole family in heaven and earth is named,

that He would grant you, according to the riches of His glory, to be strengthened with might through His Spirit in the inner man,

that Christ may dwell in your hearts through faith; that you, being rooted and grounded in love,

may be able to comprehend with all the saints what is the width and length and depth and height—

to know the love of Christ which passes knowledge; that you may be filled with all the fullness of God.

Ephesians 3:14-19

In the third chapter of Ephesians, Paul is overcome with the joy of his salvation and bows his knees to God in worship. Then he goes on to pray for the rest of the body of Christ, that the Holy Spirit would strengthen us in our inner man, that our faith in Jesus would be strong, and that we would be rooted and grounded in love. He says that the love of God goes beyond any thought.

We need to pray that our kids know how much God loves them. Then they will have the strength to resist temptation. When they understand that His love for them is beyond their ability to reason it out, they are "filled with all the fullness of God" and able to resist any temptation the enemy throws at them. Like fish that are well fed and refuse the worm on the hook; if kids are full of God's love, they will have no appetite for the bait of temptation. They will be satisfied in God's love, and sin will have no power over them.

The Power of Grace

For the grace of God that brings salvation has appeared to all men,

teaching us that, denying ungodliness and worldly lusts, we should live soberly, righteously, and godly in the present age.

Titus 2:11,12

One of the most important things you can pray for kids is for them to appreciate and appropriate the grace of God, because the grace of God teaches us to live godly lives. We couldn't get saved without God's grace, and we cannot live righteously in this world without His grace.

The Greek word for "grace" is *charis,* and it means "the divine influence upon the heart, and its reflection in the life."[1] We can pray for our kids to walk with God's influence ruling their hearts and manifesting in their thinking and behavior, that His grace will "teach" them to live holy lives in this world.

It is interesting that the Charismatic Movement is all about the gifts of the Holy Spirit and His supernatural power. In 1 Corinthians 12:1, the Greek word for "spiritual gifts" is *charisma,* and the root word is *charis,* or grace. Charismatic believers readily understand and receive the power of the Holy Spirit to operate in spiritual gifts and Holy Ghost power, but the Greek language makes it clear that the spiritual gifts are the result (*ma*) of grace (*charis*).[2] The supernatural power of God *is* His grace, when we are working a miracle—or refusing to fall to temptation. The Word of God is telling us that God's grace is what gives us the ability to resist temptation and live by the Word and the Spirit.

We need to pray that the mark of God's grace will be upon our kids in every area of their lives, especially when they are faced with a temptation that promises to reward them with great pleasure. We can pray that God's grace will fill them to overflowing when they face those situations, that His divine influence will cause them to pray in the Spirit to appropriate His grace and overcome. We can also pray that the Holy Spirit's divine influence will give them the wisdom to know that short-term pleasure brings destruction into their lives, but obeying God's Word and Spirit brings everlasting joy and prosperity.

Prayer for Strength

Father, in Jesus' name we ask You to strengthen our kids with extraordinary might in their inner man. Fill them with the revelation of Your love for them, that they will trust You to lead them and guide them in whatever circumstances they face. As they go into this evil world and encounter temptation to sin from their flesh or the enemy, give them the supernatural power of Your grace to resist and overcome. We pray that they will always be dressed in Your armor, Father, to stand against all the wiles and extinguish every fiery dart of the devil. Remind them that with every temptation they face, You have provided a way of escape. We pray and believe that they will see that way of escape and prove to be more than conquerors in Your name. Thank You that today and every day their hearts and minds are focused on Jesus, the author and finisher of their faith, and they walk steadfastly in Your Word and by the leading of Your Holy Spirit. We praise You and thank You for their great victories over temptation! In Jesus' name we pray, amen.

Endnotes

1

Wisdom

[1] James Strong, *Exhaustive Concordance of the Bible,* "Hebrew and Chaldee Dictionary," (Nashville, TN: Thomas Nelson Publishers, 1984), #8050.

3

Favor of God

[1] James Strong, *Exhaustive Concordance of the Bible,* "Hebrew and Chaldee Dictionary," (Nashville, TN: Thomas Nelson Publishers, 1984), #5375.

[2] Ibid., #6440.

[3] Kate McVeigh, *The Blessing of Favor* (Tulsa: Harrison House Publishers, copyright 2003).

7

Strength To Resist Temptation

[1] James Strong, *Exhaustive Concordance of the Bible,* "Greek Dictionary of the New Testament," (Nashville, TN: Thomas Nelson Publishers, 1984), #5485.

[2] Spiros Zhodiates, *The Complete Word Study Dictionary: New Testament,* (Chattanooga, TN: AMG Publishers, 1992) p. 1471.

Prayer of Salvation

God loves you—no matter who you are, no matter what your past. God loves you so much that He gave His one and only begotten Son for you. The Bible tells us that "...whoever believes in him shall not perish but have eternal life" (John 3:16 NIV). Jesus laid down His life and rose again so that we could spend eternity with Him in heaven and experience His absolute best on earth. If you would like to receive Jesus into your life, say the following prayer out loud and mean it from your heart.

Heavenly Father, I come to You admitting that I am a sinner. Right now, I choose to turn away from sin, and I ask You to cleanse me of all unrighteousness. I believe that Your Son, Jesus, died on the cross to take away my sins. I also believe that He rose again from the dead so that I might be forgiven of my sins and made righteous through faith in Him. I call upon the name of Jesus Christ to be the Savior and Lord of my life. Jesus, I choose to follow You and ask that You fill me with the power of the Holy Spirit. I declare that right now I am a child of God. I am free from sin and full of the righteousness of God. I am saved in Jesus' name. Amen.

If you prayed this prayer to receive Jesus Christ as your Savior for the first time, please contact us on the Web at **www.harrisonhouse.com** to receive a free book.

Or you may write to us at:

Harrison House
P.O. Box 35035
Tulsa, Oklahoma 74153

Meet Blaine Bartel

Blaine Bartel is one of America's premiere leadership specialists. Blaine served as Oneighty®'s Youth Pastor for 7 years, helping it become America's largest local church youth ministry, reaching more than 2,500 students each week. He is now the National Director of Oneighty® and Associate Pastor of 12,000-member Church On The Move in Tulsa, Oklahoma. Blaine has served under his Pastor and mentor, Willie George, for more than 20 years. God has uniquely gifted him to teach local church staff and workers to thrive while faithfully serving the vision of their leader. Known for his creativity and respected for his achievement, Blaine uses the Thrive audio resource to equip thousands of church and youth leaders each month with principles, ideas, and strategies that work.

past: Came to Christ at age 16 on the heels of the Jesus movement. While in pursuit of a professional freestyle skiing career, answered God's call to reach young people. Developed and hosted groundbreaking television series, *Fire by Nite*. Planted and pastored a growing church in Colorado Springs.

passion: Summed up in three simple words, "Serving America's Future." Blaine's life quest is "to relevantly introduce the person of Jesus Christ to each new generation of young people, leaving footprints for future leaders to follow."

personal: Still madly in love with his wife and partner of 24 years, Cathy. Raising 3 boys who love God: Jeremy—20, Dillon—18, Brock—16. Avid hockey player and fan, with a rather impressive Gretzky memorabilia collection.

To contact Blaine Bartel, please write to:
Blaine Bartel • Serving America's Future
P.O. Box 691923 • Tulsa, OK 74169

E-mail: bbartel@churchonthemove.com

Or visit him on his Web site at: www.blainebartel.com

To contact Oneighty®, please write to:

Oneighty®
P.O. Box 770 • Tulsa, OK 74101
www.Oneighty.com

Other Books by Blaine Bartel

Ten Rules of Youth Ministry and Why Oneighty® Breaks Them All

Oneighty® Devotional

the **big black book** for parents

every teenager's **little black book** of God's guarantees

every teenager's **little black book** on reaching your dreams

every teenager's **little black book** on how to get along with your parents

every teenager's **little black book** for athletes

every teenager's **little black book** on how to win a friend to Christ

every teenager's **little black book** on sex and dating

every teenager's **little black book** on cash

every teenager's **little black book** on cool

every teenager's **little black book** of hard to find information

little black book for graduates

For more information on the *little black book* series
please visit our Web site at: **www.littleblackbooks.info**

These books are available from your local bookstore
or by visiting www.harrisonhouse.com.

The Harrison House Vision

Proclaiming the truth and the power
Of the Gospel of Jesus Christ
With excellence;

Challenging Christians to
Live victoriously,
Grow spiritually,
Know God intimately.